Simply Sensational Slow Cooking

With Debra Murray

ACKNOWLEDGEMENTS

This cookbook took the efforts of many talented people, without them, I would not have been able to make this dream come true.

First, I would like to thank my husband Martin and my daughter Nevar, without your never-ending love and patience, I would not have a job I adore.

I want to thank my mother and father for such a wonderful childhood.

My most sincere thanks to Chef Wolfgang Puck. I cannot thank you enough for the opportunity to have this wonderful career and letting me share the set with you. Thank

you for all the laughter, I adore you as a chef and as a person.

Many thanks to Sydney Silverman and Mike Sanseverino, you are the nicest people one could work for.

Thanks to Marian Getz. It is a true honor to work with you.

I would also like to thank Jonathan Schwartz for your hard work and patience, and Daniel Koren for turning my collection of family recipes into a fabulous book.

Thanks to Chris Davis and his assistant Yildred Tortosa for taking these wonderful photographs, they are pieces of art as they truly capture the essence of my cooking.

I would also like to thank Nevar Murray and Tracy Ferguson for your art direction.

Special thanks to Christina Chancey for your brilliant food styling.

INTRODUCTION

Among my most vivid childhood memories in Austria are the wonderful dishes my mother and grandmother cooked. The enchanting aromas that filled our kitchen made our house a home. Using the best-quality, locally grown (often from our own garden), seasonal ingredients and their own home-style expertise, they put a lot of love into every meal. That love, along with all the delicious flavors, helped inspire me to pursue cooking myself and to spend my life sharing good food with others.

Times have changed. Nowadays, in this age of two-career couples, it almost seems a rarity to have one parent at home preparing meals. Many families find it harder to put a home-cooked dinner on the table each evening.

Strangely enough, a popular appliance of the past few decades, the slow cooker actually makes it possible to enjoy the types of evening main courses my mother and grandmother prepared. They often made stews, soups, casseroles or braises that cooked slowly in the oven or over a low fire, both of which required a watchful cook nearby. The slow cooker requires very little effort in the morning and allows you to come home to a warm, nutritious meal and a home filled with delicious aromas.

I know that Debra Murray's collection of slow cooker recipes will give you that kind of satisfaction. She has been my assistant at the Home Shopping Network for almost ten years, and I've witnessed time after time her passion for good cooking and for the kinds of quality appliances that can make anyone a better cook. The slow cooker is one of her favorite appliances, and I have urged her to share her favorite recipes with as many people as possible through this book.

A talented cook in her own right, Debra shares my WELL (Wolfgang's Eat, Love, Live!™) philosophy of good cooking and warm hospitality. I believe everyone should use the freshest, all-natural ingredients they can find, locally grown, produced using sustainable humane methods and organic whenever possible. As I learned long ago alongside my mother and grandmother, you should always put lots of love into everything you cook.

TABLE OF CONTENTS

Appetizers & Beverages
Page 9

Breakfast & Brunch
Page 28

Soups & Stews
Page 42

Side Dishes
Page 54

TABLE OF CONTENTS

Beef & Ground Beef Meals
Page 74

Chicken & Turkey Meals
Page 98

Pork & Sausage Meals
Page 113

Desserts
Page 127

SECRETS TO SLOW COOKING

Slow cookers have become one of the most popular kitchen appliances. They allow incredible results with minimal effort. For over 30 years, I have exchanged recipes with stay-at-home moms, senior citizens, working professionals, and even people from my painting class. Everyone adores slow cookers, and I am one of them.

Here are a few of my secrets to help you achieve excellent results:

- Place ingredients into the slow cooker according to their density; dense textures on the bottom, soft textures on top.

- Remove skin from poultry when using a slow cooker. It never gets crunchy so why have the extra calories.

- Use bone-in meats as the bones will enhance the flavor of the stock.

- You might ask where are the fish or seafood recipes? The texture of seafood prepared in a slow cooker is not ideal so I prefer to grill or steam them.

- Some types of rice lose texture in the slow cooker, use Arborio rice, wild rice and brown rice.

- As a thickening agent, I use quick cook tapioca instead of cornstarch or flour.

- The slow cooker is ideal for any recipe that calls for a water bath like cheesecake.

- When baking, you can use a baking form placed inside the slow cooker.

Enjoy!

Deb

APPETIZERS & BEVERAGES

Let's Get This Party Started...

HOT CHICKEN WINGS

Ingredients:

3 pounds chicken wings, drumettes preferred

1 small envelope ranch dressing

Peanut oil for deep frying

Sauce:

¼ cup unsalted butter

½ cup Louisiana-style hot sauce

2 teaspoons cider vinegar

1 teaspoon soy sauce

2 tablespoons ketchup

1. Wash wings, pat dry and place in a zipper bag.
2. Add ranch dressing to zipper bag and toss well. Refrigerate overnight.
3. The next day, fry wings at 375 degrees for 9 minutes.
4. Drain wings on paper towels.
5. In a saucepan, heat butter and hot sauce.
6. Whisk in remaining sauce ingredients. Do not allow to boil.
7. Set slow cooker on warm mode.
8. Toss wings with sauce and add to crockery.

Deb's Tip:
Serve with celery, carrots and my blue cheese dressing; the recipe is on page 13.

TUSCAN WINGS

Ingredients:

2 pounds chicken wings, drumettes preferred

1 lemon, juice and zest

1 tablespoon steakhouse seasoning

1 tablespoon fresh rosemary leaves or 1 teaspoon dried rosemary leaves

1 teaspoon fresh thyme or ½ teaspoon dried thyme

Non-stick cooking spray

1. Place chicken, lemon, rosemary and thyme in a zipper bag.
2. Seal bag, shake well and refrigerate overnight.
3. The next day, preheat broiler and place oven rack in second highest position.
4. Use parchment paper to cover a shallow pan.
5. Spread chicken wings on paper and coat with steakhouse seasoning.
6. Broil wings for 10 minutes on each side.
7. Spray crockery with non-stick spray.
8. Transfer wings to crockery.
9. Set slow cooker on warm mode.

BLUE CHEESE DRESSING

Ingredients:

4 ounces blue cheese

1 small shallot, minced

1 garlic clove, minced

¼ teaspoon kosher or sea salt

½ teaspoon freshly ground pepper

1 teaspoon red wine vinegar

1 teaspoon fresh lemon juice

½ cup mayonnaise

1 tablespoon flat-leaf Italian parsley

1 cup sour cream

1. In a small microwaveable glass container, place 2 ounces of blue cheese, shallots and garlic.
2. Microwave 45 seconds on high until shallots and garlic are cooked. The cheese should be melted as well. Let cool.
3. Mix remaining ingredients with an Immersion blender or a food processor.
4. Combine all ingredients. Mix well.

Deb's Tip:
This recipe also makes an amazing salad dressing.

MULLED APPLE CIDER

Ingredients:

1 gallon apple cider or apple juice

1 cup brown sugar

1 orange, cut into ½-inch rings

5 cinnamon sticks

1 slice fresh ginger

2 whole allspice berries

1 star anise

½ teaspoon nutmeg

1 cup apple brandy

1. Place all ingredients into crockery. Cover.
2. Slow cook 2 hours on high or 4 hours on low.

Deb's Tip:
For a color twist, substitute cranberry or pomegranate juice for the apple cider.

CROWD-PLEASING PIZZA FONDUE

Makes 25 to 30 servings

Ingredients:

1 pound Italian sausage, casings removed

1 pound ground beef

1 cup onions, chopped

3 garlic cloves, minced

1 pound mushrooms, sliced

1 green bell pepper, diced

1 red bell pepper, diced

1 package (3½ ounces) pepperoni, diced

3 teaspoons Italian seasoning

2 jars (28 ounces each) pasta sauce

1 can (2¼ ounces) black olives, sliced

1. In a sauté pan, cook sausage and drain fat.
2. Transfer to crockery.
3. In the same pan, cook ground beef and drain fat.
4. Transfer to crockery.
5. Add remaining ingredients to crockery. Cover.
6. Slow cook 2 hours on high or 4 hours on low.

Deb's Tip:
Serve with fried Mozzarella sticks,
fried ravioli, or warm breadsticks.

HOT BOILED PEANUTS

Ingredients:

5 cups raw peanuts, in shell
½ cup salt
9 cups water

1. Wash peanuts until water is clear.
2. Place into crockery.
3. Stir in salt and water to crockery. Cover.
4. Slow cook 6 hours on high.
5. If necessary, add additional water to keep nuts covered during slow cooking.

Deb's Tip:
Like it hot? Add a pinch of crushed red pepper flakes
to the crockery.

MIX TRICKS

Ingredients:

4 cups multi-grain cereal

4 cups oat cereal

3 cups salted pretzel sticks

16 ounces dry roasted peanuts

½ cup salted butter, melted

1 teaspoon garlic salt

1 teaspoon celery salt

1 teaspoon seasoned salt

½ teaspoon cayenne pepper

2 tablespoons Parmesan cheese, grated

1. Toss cereals, pretzels and nuts into crockery.
2. Drizzle with butter, salts, cayenne pepper and cheese. Mix well. Cover.
3. Slow cook 4 hours on low.
4. Remove lid and cook uncovered for an additional 30 minutes.
5. Stir several times during process.

RANCH NUTS

Ingredients:

Non-stick cooking spray
2 pounds of peanuts or walnuts
3 tablespoons ranch seasoning
Pinch of cayenne pepper

1. Spray crockery with non-stick spray.
2. Toss ingredients into crockery. Cover.
3. Slow cook 15 minutes on high.
4. Reduce heat to low and cook for an additional 2 hours.
5. Remove lid and stir.
6. Cook for an additional 30 minutes, uncovered, on high.
7. Transfer nuts to a baking tray.
8. Cool thoroughly.
9. Store in an airtight container.

Deb's Tip:
Substitute dry Italian dressing or chili seasoning for the ranch dressing.

SPINACH DIP

Ingredients:

Non-stick cooking spray

2 packages (8 ounces each) cream cheese

1 envelope dry vegetable soup mix

½ cup Parmesan cheese, grated

2 cans artichoke hearts, drained and quartered

2 packages (10 ounces each) spinach, thawed and drained

1. Spray crockery with non-stick spray.
2. Using an electric mixer on low, blend cream cheese, soup mix and Parmesan.
3. Add artichoke hearts and spinach. Mix well.
4. Place ingredients into crockery. Cover.
5. Slow cook 1½ hours on high or 3 hours on low.
6. Stir before serving.

Deb's Tip:
Like seafood? Fold in 1 pound of lump blue crab
just before serving.

MAMA MIA MEATBALLS

Makes 10 to 12 servings

Ingredients:

32 ounces spaghetti sauce

4 pounds lean ground beef

1 cup freshly ground bread crumbs or day-old French bread

1 cup beef or chicken stock

Olive oil

1 medium onion, chopped

3 garlic cloves, minced

1 teaspoon garlic salt

½ teaspoon onion powder

1 tablespoon parsley flakes

1 tablespoon Italian herbs

½ cup Parmesan cheese, grated

½ teaspoon ground pepper

½ teaspoon salt

2 large eggs

1. Pour spaghetti sauce into crockery. Cover.
2. In a large bowl, mix meat, bread crumbs and enough stock to cover bread.
3. In a small sauté pan, heat 2 tablespoons of oil over medium heat.
4. Add onions and cook until translucent.
5. Add garlic and cook for an additional 1 minute. Let cool.
6. Transfer cooled onions and garlic to the meat mixture.
7. Add remaining ingredients. Mix well.
8. Using a 2-ounce sized ice cream scoop, form meatballs.
9. In a pan, heat oil and sauté meatballs.
10. Transfer to hot spaghetti sauce in crockery. Cover.
11. Slow cook for an additional 4 hours on high or 8 hours on low.

Deb's Tip:
For a twist, try barbecue sauce instead of spaghetti sauce.

SPICY ITALIAN BEEF SANDWICHES

Ingredients:

4 pound roast beef, eye of round, rump roast or top round

2 teaspoons kosher salt

1 teaspoon ground pepper

1 tablespoon dry Italian seasoning

1 jar (7 ounces) pepperoncini with juice

1 medium onion, sliced ¼-inch thick

2 green bell peppers, julienned

½ teaspoon beef bouillon

10 slices Mozzarella cheese

6 to 8 Italian rolls

1. Rub roast beef with salt, pepper and Italian seasoning.
2. Transfer to crockery. Cover.
3. Slow cook 4 hours on high or 8 hours on low.
4. In the last hour of cooking, remove beef.
5. Slice beef and return to crockery.
6. Add pepperoncini and its juice, onions, bell peppers and bouillon. Cover.
7. Let beef cook for remaining 1 hour.
8. Serve on rolls with cheese. Use meat juices for dipping.

HOT WHITE CHOCOLATE

Ingredients:

4 cups half-and-half or heavy cream

1 teaspoon vanilla

1½ cups white chocolate baking chips

1 cup white chocolate liqueur

Vanilla-flavored whipped topping

Nutmeg

1. Place cream, vanilla, baking chips and liqueur into crockery. Cover.
2. Slow cook 2 hours on low.
3. Whisk every 30 minutes.
4. Serve with whipped topping.
5. Garnish with nutmeg.

Deb's Tip:
For a peppermint twist, add peppermint extract or peppermint liqueur. Garnish with a peppermint stick.

BREAKFAST & BRUNCH

Worth Waking Up For...

WAKE-UP BAKE

Ingredients:

Non-stick cooking spray

1 package (20 ounces) cooked potatoes, thinly sliced

3 cups Swiss cheese, shredded

12 ounces deli ham, thinly sliced

1½ cups onions, chopped

1 large green bell pepper, chopped

1 large yellow or red bell pepper, chopped

8 ounces mushrooms, sliced

2 medium tomatoes, sliced

12 large eggs

2½ cups milk

½ teaspoon salt

¼ teaspoon ground pepper

¼ cup Parmesan cheese, shredded

1. Spray crockery with non-stick spray.
2. Layer all ingredients except eggs, milk, salt and pepper in crockery.
3. In a large bowl, beat eggs.
4. Combine eggs, milk, salt and pepper.
5. Pour egg mixture over potatoes in crockery.
6. Sprinkle with Parmesan. Cover.
7. Slow cook 4 hours on high or 8 hours on low.

BRUNCH BAKE

Ingredients:

Non-stick cooking spray

1 pound breakfast sausage, maple or sage flavored, cooked and drained

1 package (32 ounces) frozen potato hash browns

1 green bell pepper, diced

½ cup onions, diced

4 large eggs

1 cup buttermilk baking mix

2 cups Cheddar cheese, shredded

3 cups milk

1. Spray crockery with non-stick spray.
2. In a large bowl, toss sausage, potatoes, peppers and onions.
3. Transfer to crockery.
4. In a separate bowl, combine eggs, baking mix, cheese and milk.
5. Pour over sausage mixture. Cover.
6. Slow cook 2 hours on high or 4 hours or low.

STUFFED FRENCH TOAST

Makes 10 to 12 servings

Ingredients:

Non-stick cooking spray
1 package (4 ounces) berry-flavored cream cheese
¼ cup butter
2 tablespoons powdered sugar
2 cups strawberries or raspberries, fresh or frozen
1 cup raspberry preserves
¼ cup raspberry-flavored liqueur
12 slices white bread

Custard:

4 large eggs or 1 cup egg substitute
1 cup cream
1 tablespoon vanilla
¼ cup sugar

Topping:

½ cup cornflakes, crushed
½ cup almonds, slivered

1. Spray crockery with non-stick spray.
2. In a bowl, mix cream cheese, butter and powdered sugar until smooth.
3. In a separate bowl, blend berries, preserves and liqueur.
4. Place 4 pieces of bread into crockery and top with cream cheese mixture.
5. Add an additional 4 slices of bread and top with berry mixture.
6. Layer with 4 more slices of bread.
7. In a separate bowl, combine custard ingredients and pour over bread.
8. Top with cornflakes and almonds. Cover.
9. Slow cook 2 hours on high or 4 hours on low.

Deb's Tip:
To make this extra special, dust with powdered
sugar and serve with fresh berries.

LOW-FAT STRATA

Ingredients:

Non-stick cooking spray

8 cups whole-grain bread, cubed

1 cup reduced-fat Mozzarella or Cheddar cheese, shredded

1 pound bulk turkey breakfast sausage, cooked and crumbled

½ cup onions, diced

1 cup broccoli flowerets

2 cups egg substitute

3 cups low-fat milk

1 teaspoon salt

½ teaspoon dry mustard

½ cup Parmesan cheese, grated

1. Spray crockery with non-stick spray.
2. In a bowl, combine all ingredients, except Parmesan.
3. Transfer to crockery and top with Parmesan. Cover.
4. Slow cook 4 hours on high or 8 hours on low.

Deb's Tip:
Let strata cook overnight and wake up
to a delicious breakfast.

SAUSAGE STRATA

Ingredients:

Non-stick cooking spray

8 cups French bread, crusts removed, diced

2 pounds Kielbasa, cut into ½-inch slices, then quartered

1 large red bell pepper, diced

½ cup onions, diced

1 cup sharp Cheddar cheese, shredded

6 large eggs, beaten

1 teaspoon salt

1 teaspoon ground pepper

3 cups milk

1. Spray crockery with non-stick spray.
2. In a bowl, combine all ingredients and transfer to crockery. Cover.
3. Slow cook 4 hours on high or 8 hours on low.

Deb's Tip:
If you like it with a little kick, try using Andouille sausage instead of Kielbasa.

RAINY-DAY QUICHE

Ingredients:

Non-stick cooking spray

1 refrigerator pie crust

6 large eggs

1½ cups heavy cream

1 teaspoon salt

½ teaspoon ground pepper

1 cup Cheddar cheese, shredded

1 cup breakfast sausage, cooked and crumbled

Hot sauce

Parsley, chopped

1. Spray crockery with non-stick spray.
2. Unroll pie crust and spread across bottom of crockery, reaching ends.
3. Slow cook, uncovered, for 30 minutes on high.
4. In a bowl, beat eggs.
5. Add cream, salt and pepper to bowl. Mix well.
6. Pour egg mixture over crust and sprinkle with cheese and sausage.
7. Top with hot sauce and parsley. Cover.
8. Slow cook 2 hours on high.

Deb's Tip:
Cut the quiche into squares and take it with you as a breakast-to-go.

ZESTY BANANA BREAD

Makes 8 servings

Ingredients:

Non-stick cooking spray

2 ripe bananas, peeled

1 package (15.4 ounces) nut flavored quick bread

¾ cup water

½ cup egg substitute

1 teaspoon orange zest

2 tablespoons flaxseed oil

½ cup walnuts, chopped

1. Spray crockery with non-stick spray.
2. In a large bowl, mash bananas.
3. Add remaining ingredients, except walnuts, to bowl. Mix well.
4. Transfer to crockery and top with walnuts. Cover.
5. Slow cook 1 hour on high.

Deb's Tip:
To make it even more decadent, top the banana
bread with cream cheese or peanut butter.

COWBOY CASSEROLE

Ingredients:

1 package (32 ounces) frozen potato hash browns

1 pound extra-lean ham, diced

1 medium onion, diced

1 medium green bell pepper, diced

1½ cups Monterey Jack or Cheddar cheese, shredded

12 large eggs

1 cup skim milk

1 teaspoon salt

1 teaspoon ground pepper

1. Cover bottom of crockery with hash browns.
2. Layer some ham, onions, green pepper and cheese.
3. Repeat layering three times and cover top with cheese.
4. In a bowl, beat eggs, milk, salt and pepper.
5. Pour mixture into crockery. Cover.
6. Slow cook 10 hours on low.

Deb's Tip:
Add a cup of corn to this dish to get
a different texture.

HARD COOKED EGGS

Ingredients:

12 large eggs
Water

1. Place chilled eggs into crockery.
2. Cover with lukewarm water.
3. Slow cook 4 hours on low.
4. Drain water and remove eggs from crockery.
5. Place eggs in a bowl and cover with ice.
6. Let eggs cool.
7. Drain and serve.

SOUPS & STEWS

To Cuddle Up With...

BEEF & VEGETABLE SOUP

Makes 6 to 8 servings

Ingredients:

2 pounds beef shanks, cross-cut

4 cups beef or vegetable stock

1 teaspoon salt

1½ teaspoons Worcestershire sauce

Pinch of ground pepper

2 teaspoons dried parsley flakes

1 onion, chopped

1 package (8 ounces) frozen cut green beans

1 cup celery, chopped

1 cup carrots, peeled and sliced

1 cup potatoes, peeled and diced

1 can (16 ounces) petite diced tomatoes

1 cup fresh or frozen corn

1. In a sauté pan, brown beef shanks.
2. Transfer beef and remaining ingredients to crockery. Cover.
3. Slow cook 4 hours on high or 8 hours on low.
4. Remove shanks and chop meat from bones.
5. Stir into soup and serve.

Deb's Tip:
Put spinach tortellini in each bowl of soup and drizzle with basil oil before serving.

PACIFIC RIM CHICKEN SOUP

Ingredients:

1 pound chicken, boneless, skinless, cut in 1-inch pieces

1 small leek, white portion only

2 stalks celery, chopped

2 garlic cloves, minced

1 teaspoon freshly grated ginger

1 tablespoon soy sauce

8 cups chicken stock

1 cup coleslaw, shredded cabbage or matchstick carrots

2 cups stir-fry vegetables, fresh or frozen

2 ounces somen or rice noodles

1 small green onion, chopped

1. Place all ingredients, except vegetables and noodles, into crockery. Cover.
2. Slow cook 2 hours on high or 4 hours on low.
3. About 20 minutes before serving, add vegetables and noodles to crockery.
4. Top with green onions and serve.

Deb's Tip:
If I have it on hand, I add a teaspoon of
either green chili paste or fresh white miso.

THIS STEW'S FOR YOU

Makes 8 servings

Ingredients:

2 tablespoons extra-virgin olive oil

2 pounds lean beef, cut into 1-inch cubes

1 tablespoon flour

1 teaspoon salt

½ teaspoon ground pepper

1 pound small red potatoes, quartered

1 package (16 ounces) frozen pearl onions

1 package (16 ounces) baby carrots

1 can golden mushroom soup

1 can (14½ ounces) petite diced tomatoes

2 sprigs of thyme

1. Coat beef with flour, salt and pepper.
2. In a large sauté pan, heat oil over medium heat.
3. Brown beef on all sides and transfer to crockery.
4. Add remaining ingredients to crockery. Cover.
5. Slow cook 5 hours on high or 10 hours on low.

Deb's Tip:
I love root vegetables; try celery root
instead of potatoes.

FRENCH ONION SOUP

Makes 8 to 10 servings

Ingredients:

2 tablespoons salted butter

4 large sweet onions, thinly sliced

1 teaspoon sugar

1 tablespoon sweet vermouth

1 tablespoon Worcestershire sauce

½ teaspoon ground pepper

1 Bay leaf

8 cups beef stock

1. In a sauté pan, heat butter over medium heat.
2. Add onions and sugar to sauté pan. Cook until onions are caramelized.
3. Transfer onions to crockery.
4. Deglaze sauté pan with the vermouth and pour into crockery.
5. Add remaining ingredients to crockery. Cover.
6. Slow cook 4 hours on high or 8 hours on low.
7. Remove bay leaf before serving.

Deb's Tip:
Top this soup with a Crostini; the recipe
is on the next page.

CROSTINI

Ingredients:

1 loaf French or Italian bread

Olive oil

Swiss or Provolone cheese slices

1. Move oven rack closest to broiler.
2. Preheat broiler.
3. Slice bread on the diagonal.
4. Place bread on a large baking sheet lined with parchment paper.
5. Brush each side of the bread with oil.
6. Toast each side until lightly browned.
7. Top with cheese.
8. Broil until bubbly.

SIRLOIN CHILI SUPREME

Ingredients:

1 pound beef sirloin, boneless, trimmed, cut into 1-inch pieces

1 pound pork, trimmed, cut into 1-inch pieces

1 green bell pepper, diced

1 cup onions, diced

3 garlic cloves, minced

1 package (1¼ ounces) chili seasoning

1 teaspoon salt

½ teaspoon ground pepper

1 can (15 ounces) dark red kidney beans

1 can (28 ounces) diced tomatoes

1 can (10 ounces) tomatoes with green chilies and lime

1 can (8 ounces) tomato sauce

1. Place all ingredients into crockery. Cover.
2. Slow cook 4 hours on high or 8 hours on low.

Deb's Tip:
Garnish with sour cream, shredded Cheddar cheese, and chopped green onions.

WHITE CHILI

Ingredients:

5 cups cooked chicken or turkey, shredded or ground

3 cups chicken stock

1 envelope (1¼ ounces) chili seasoning

1 cup onions, diced

2 garlic cloves, minced

1 green chili, diced, seeds and membrane removed

1 tablespoon fresh cilantro, chopped

2 cans (15½ ounces each) great northern beans, drained

1 can (10¾ ounces) cream of chicken soup

1. Place all ingredients into crockery. Cover.
2. Slow cook 4 hours on high or 8 hours on low.

Deb's Tip:
Garnish with sour cream, shredded Cheddar cheese, and chopped green onions.

CHILI VERDE

Ingredients:

2 dried chilies, seeded and chopped

1 cup chicken stock

1 green chili, coarsely chopped

1 can (4 ounces) green chilies, diced

1 jalapeno, diced, seeds and membrane removed

1 onion, coarsely chopped

4 garlic cloves, minced

7 tomatillos

3 pounds pork, cubed

1 bundle cilantro, stems removed, chopped

1 teaspoon cumin

1 teaspoon salt

1 teaspoon ground pepper

Sour cream

1. In a food processor, purée dried chilies and chicken stock. Transfer to crockery.
2. Add remaining ingredients, except sour cream, to crockery. Cover.
3. Slow cook 4 hours on high or 8 hours on low.
4. Serve with sour cream.

SIDE DISHES

These Will Steal The Show...

EASY SCALLOPED POTATOES

Ingredients:

¼ cup salted butter

1 small onion, thinly sliced

2 tablespoons flour

1½ cups heavy cream

1 teaspoon salt

1 teaspoon ground pepper

½ teaspoon dry mustard

3 Russet potatoes, sliced ¼-inch thick

Non-stick cooking spray

6 slices deli ham, chopped

2 tablespoons freshly chopped chives or 1 teaspoon dried chives

1. In a sauté pan, heat butter and cook onions until tender.
2. In a bowl, dissolve flour in cream and add seasonings.
3. Transfer cream mixture to sauté pan. Whisk until smooth.
4. Spray crockery with non-stick spray.
5. Layer potatoes in crockery.
6. Sprinkle ham over potatoes and pour cream mixture into crockery.
7. Top with chives. Cover.
8. Slow cook 3 hours on high or 6 hours on low.

Deb's Tip:
Convert this dish to au gratin by omitting the ham
and adding a cup of shredded Gruyere or Swiss cheese.

GREEN BEAN CASSEROLE

Ingredients:

3 pounds fresh green beans, washed, stem tips removed

2 medium sweet onions, thinly sliced

2 tablespoons extra-virgin olive oil

1½ cups mushrooms, sliced

1 tablespoon salted butter

1 teaspoon ground pepper

1½ teaspoons kosher salt

1 tablespoon sherry

1 package (8 ounces) instant brown gravy

2 cans (10¾ ounces each) cream of mushroom soup

1 can french fried onions

1. Place all ingredients, except onions, into crockery. Cover.
2. Slow cook 2 hours on high or 4 hours on low.
3. Top with onions during the last 30 minutes of cooking.

SQUASH CASSEROLE

Ingredients:

Non-stick cooking spray

2 large sweet onions, chopped

6 large crookneck squash, cut into 1-inch pieces

6 tablespoons salted butter, melted

1½ teaspoons salt

1 teaspoon ground pepper

1¼ cups Swiss cheese, shredded

1¼ cups Parmesan cheese, shredded

1½ cups Cheddar cheese, shredded

1 sleeve buttery crackers

1 tablespoon parsley

1. Spray crockery with non-stick spray.
2. Place onions, squash and 3 tablespoons melted butter into crockery.
3. Add salt, pepper and shredded cheeses. Mix well.
4. Crush crackers and mix with remaining butter and parsley.
5. Pour into crockery. Cover.
6. Slow cook 3 hours on low.

SPAGHETTI SQUASH

Ingredients:

1 large spaghetti squash, cut horizontally, seeds removed

2 tablespoons salted butter

Pinch of salt and ground pepper

1. Place spaghetti squash into crockery.
2. Put a tablespoon of butter in each squash half.
3. Sprinkle with salt and pepper. Cover.
4. Slow cook 4 hours on high.
5. Using a spoon, remove squash from shell and serve.

Deb's Tip:
Spaghetti squash is an excellent gluten-free substitute for pasta.

ROASTED ROOT VEGGIES

Ingredients:

3 medium Russet potatoes, peeled, cut into 1-inch pieces

2 sweet potatoes, peeled, cut into 1-inch pieces

3 medium parsnips, peeled, cut into 1-inch pieces

1 medium onion, quartered

1 tablespoon extra-virgin olive oil

1 teaspoon balsamic vinegar

1 teaspoon kosher salt

1 teaspoon ground pepper

1 teaspoon fresh thyme leaves

1. Place vegetables into crockery.
2. In a bowl, combine remaining ingredients and pour over vegetables. Cover.
3. Slow cook 8 hours on low.

MIGHTY MAC

Ingredients:

1 package (16 ounces) elbow macaroni

Non-stick cooking spray

3 cups mild Cheddar cheese, shredded

1 can evaporated milk

1½ cups milk

¼ cup salted butter

Pinch of salt and ground pepper

1. Cook macaroni according to package directions, subtracting 2 minutes from cooking time.
2. Spray crockery with non-stick spray.
3. In a bowl, combine macaroni with remaining ingredients. Mix well.
4. Transfer to crockery. Cover.
5. Slow cook 30 minutes on high.
6. Reduce to low and cook for an additional 2 hours.

Deb's Tip:
For a more robust flavor, try 1 cup of Parmesan with 2 cups of mild Cheddar cheese.

STUFFED ARTICHOKES

Ingredients:

5 medium artichokes

Pinch of salt

6 tablespoons lemon juice

Stuffing:

½ cup extra-virgin olive oil

4 garlic cloves, minced

2 tablespoons mint leaves, chopped

2 tablespoons Italian parsley, chopped

2 cups Italian-flavored bread crumbs

1 cup Parmesan cheese, shredded

2 cups chicken stock

1. Remove artichoke stems and outer leaves.
2. Use scissors to cut off 1-inch tops.
3. Place artichokes in a bowl of salted water and add 2 tablespoons lemon juice.
4. In a small sauté pan, heat oil and cook garlic until tender; do not brown.
5. For the stuffing, combine herbs, bread crumbs, garlic and cheese.
6. Add 2 tablespoons of lemon juice to mixture. Blend well.
7. Spread leaves apart, fill with stuffing and place upright into crockery.
8. Pour stock and remaining lemon juice over artichokes. Cover.
9. Slow cook 4 hours on high or 8 hours on low.

VEGETARIAN BAKED BEANS

Ingredients:

2 pounds dried Navy beans

5 cups vegetable stock

1 large onion, quartered

1½ cups ketchup

¼ cup maple syrup

1 cup dark brown sugar

½ cup molasses

1 tablespoon dry mustard

½ teaspoon ginger

1 teaspoon kosher salt

1. Sort and wash beans.
2. Place beans in a bowl and cover with water; let soak overnight.
3. The next day, rinse and drain beans.
4. Place beans and remaining ingredients into crockery. Cover.
5. Slow cook 8 hours on high.

Deb's Tip:
If you wish to make a more traditional version of baked beans, add 4 ounces of fried salt pork to the crockery.

BORDER BLACK BEANS

Ingredients:

2 pounds dried black beans

7 cups beef stock

1 medium onion, diced

3 garlic cloves, chopped

1 green bell pepper, chopped

1 tablespoon fresh cilantro or oregano, chopped

Pinch of sugar

1 teaspoon cumin

1 can (14½ ounces) diced tomatoes with green chilies

1. Sort and wash beans.
2. Place beans in a bowl and cover with water; let soak overnight.
3. The next day, rinse and drain beans.
4. Place beans and remaining ingredients into crockery. Cover.
5. Slow cook 4 hours on high or 8 hours on low.

Deb's Tip:
For more flavor, try soaking the black beans with
two packets of Latin seasoning added to the water.

WILD RICE DUET

Ingredients:

Non-stick cooking spray

1½ cups wild rice

1 cup brown rice

1 cup celery, diced

1 cup onions, diced

1 tablespoon sage, chopped

4 cups chicken stock

1 can (10¾ ounces) cream of chicken soup with herbs

1. Spray crockery with non-stick spray.
2. Place all ingredients into crockery. Cover.
3. Slow cook 8 hours on low.

Deb's Tip:
A pretty and delicious addition to this rice
is to add a half cup dried cranberries.

SCALLOPED CORN

Ingredients:

Non-stick cooking spray

3 boxes (8 ounces each) corn bread mix

½ cup salted butter, melted

2 large eggs, beaten

1 cup sour cream

2 cans (14¾ ounces each) creamed corn

4 cups frozen whole kernel corn

¼ teaspoon salt

¼ teaspoon ground pepper

¼ teaspoon garlic powder

1. Spray crockery with non-stick spray.
2. In a large bowl, mix ingredients and pour into crockery. Cover.
3. Slow cook 2 hours on high or 4 hours on low.

Deb's Tip:
For extra kick, add 1 tablespoon chopped green chilies.

DEB'S TOMATO SAUCE

Ingredients:

20 Roma tomatoes

2 tablespoons olive oil

1 can (6 ounces) tomato paste

1 cup onions, chopped

5 garlic cloves, chopped

1 teaspoon kosher salt

1 teaspoon garlic salt

1 teaspoon onion salt

½ teaspoon sugar

1 teaspoon dried oregano

2 sprigs of fresh thyme or ½ teaspoon dried thyme

1. Pour water to fill half of a stock pot. Bring to a boil then add tomatoes.
2. When the water comes to a second boil, drain tomatoes. Let cool.
3. Peel tomatoes, cut them in half and remove seeds.
4. In a sauté pan, heat olive oil over medium heat.
5. Add tomato paste and drained tomatoes; cook for 3 minutes.
6. Add onions and chopped garlic.
7. Cook for an additional 5 minutes, making sure the garlic does not burn.
8. Transfer to crockery. Add remaining seasonings. Cover.
9. Slow cook 2 hours on high or 4 hours on low.

YAM-GOOD ORANGE POTATOES

Makes 8 to 10 servings

Ingredients:

4 large sweet potatoes or yams, peeled, diced into 1-inch cubes

½ cup orange juice

2 tablespoons honey or brown sugar

1 teaspoon seasoning salt

1 tablespoon salted butter

1. In a bowl, combine all ingredients.
2. Transfer to crockery. Cover.
3. Slow cook 2 hours on high or 4 hours on low.

Deb's Tip:
Mash sweet potatoes and top with crumbled gingersnaps or melted marshmallows.

SLOW COOKER STUFFING

Ingredients:

1 stick salted butter or margarine

1 cup onions, finely chopped

1 cup celery, finely chopped

1 cup fresh mushrooms, sliced

1 tablespoon fresh sage, minced

¼ cup parsley, chopped

1½ teaspoons poultry seasoning

½ teaspoon salt

Pinch of ground pepper

12 cups toasted bread cubes

2 cups chicken stock

1. In a sauté pan, heat butter over medium heat.
2. Sauté onions and celery until tender.
3. Stir in mushrooms, sage, and parsley.
4. In a bowl, combine seasonings and add bread cubes. Toss well.
5. Add stock and onion mixture to bowl.
6. Pour into crockery. Cover.
7. Slow cook 2 hours on high or 4 hours on low.

Deb's Tip:
For a delicious addition, add 1 pound of cooked and crumpled sage breakfast sausage.

BEEF & GROUND BEEF MEALS

Hearty And Delicious...

BRAISED SHORT RIBS

Ingredients:

1 tablespoon olive oil

4 to 6 pound beef short ribs, cut into individual ribs

3 medium onions, chopped

4 large garlic cloves, minced

1 cup dry red wine

1 can (28 ounces) whole tomatoes with juice

2 tablespoons Worcestershire sauce

2 teaspoons rosemary leaves, chopped

½ teaspoon salt

2 cups frozen pearl onions

1 pound baby carrots, peeled

1. In a large sauté pan, heat oil over medium heat.
2. Brown ribs on each side. Transfer to crockery.
3. Place remaining ingredients into crockery. Cover.
4. Slow cook 4 hours on high or 8 hours on low.
5. Skim fat from sauce before serving.

Deb's Tip:
Serve with warm polenta.

BEEF POT ROAST

Ingredients:

¼ cup flour

½ teaspoon salt

¼ teaspoon ground pepper

3 pound beef chuck roast, boneless

1 tablespoon olive oil

8 new potatoes

8 peeled carrots, cut into 1-inch pieces

1 cup frozen pearl onions

1 tablespoon Worcestershire sauce

1 cup beef stock

2 tablespoons tomato paste

1 sprig of fresh thyme

1 bay leaf

1. Coat beef with flour, salt and pepper.
2. In a sauté pan, heat oil over medium heat.
3. Brown beef on all sides, drain fat and transfer to crockery.
4. Add potatoes, carrots and onions to crockery.
5. In a bowl, mix Worcestershire sauce, beef stock and tomato paste.
6. Pour over roast. Sprinkle with additional salt, pepper and herbs. Cover.
7. Slow cook 5 hours on high or 10 hours on low.
8. Remove bay leaf before serving.

Deb's Tip:
To dress up the sauce, add 2 tablespoons of black cherry preserves.

ROPA VIEJA (Cuban Shredded Beef)

Ingredients:

2 pound flank steak

1 cup beef stock

1 can (10 ounces) spicy tomatoes with chilies and cilantro

1 can (14 ounces) stewed tomatoes with onions and peppers

2 tablespoons capers

1. Place all ingredients into crockery. Cover.
2. Slow cook 4 hours on high or 8 hours on low.
3. Remove meat from crockery.
4. Using a fork, shred meat into long strands.
5. Return meat to crockery.
6. Mix and serve.

Deb's Tip:
Roll meat into tortillas to make a delicious burrito.

STUFFED FLANK STEAK

Ingredients:

1 flank steak (1½ to 2 pound), butterflied

1 green bell pepper, cut into strips

1 small onion, cut into strips

¼ cup Parmesan cheese, shredded

2 tablespoons olive oil

1 teaspoon Italian seasoning

1 teaspoon salt

Pinch of ground pepper

1 cup beef stock

1 can (14½ ounces) Italian seasoned stewed tomatoes

Pasta or rice

1. Open butterflied flank steak.
2. Top with bell peppers, onions and cheese.
3. Roll up steak and tie with butcher's twine.
4. Rub steak with oil, Italian seasoning, salt and pepper.
5. In a sauté pan, heat 1 tablespoon of oil and brown steak.
6. Transfer to crockery. Add stock and tomatoes. Cover.
7. Slow cook 4 hours on high or 8 hours on low.
8. Remove flank steak and cut off twine.
9. Cut flank steak into ½-inch slices.
10. Pour sauce over flank steak.
11. Serve with pasta or rice.

SWISS STEAK

Ingredients:

1 tablespoon extra-virgin olive oil

2 pound beef round steak, cut into ¾-inch slices

1 teaspoon steak seasoning

1 large sweet onion, thinly sliced

1 can (14½ ounces) diced tomatoes with juice, basil and garlic

½ cup celery, chopped

½ cup carrots, sliced

1 jar (12 ounces) beef gravy

Noodles

1. Rub beef with steak seasoning.
2. In a sauté pan, heat oil over medium heat.
3. Brown beef on both sides and transfer to crockery.
4. In the same pan, brown onions and transfer to crockery.
5. Place remaining ingredients, except noodles, into crockery. Cover.
6. Slow cook 4 hours on high or 8 hours on low.
7. Serve over noodles.

BARBECUE BEEF SANDWICHES

Makes 6 to 10 servings

Ingredients:

3 to 3½ pound beef brisket

1 medium onion, chopped

1 teaspoon chili powder

¼ cup lime juice

½ cup brown sugar

1 tablespoon Worcestershire sauce

2 garlic cloves, minced

1 can (6 ounces) tomato paste

1 bottle beer (12 ounces)

Hamburger buns

1. Trim fat from brisket and place into crockery.
2. In a large bowl, combine remaining ingredients, except buns.
3. Pour mixture over brisket. Cover.
4. Slow cook 5 hours on high or 10 hours on low.
5. Remove brisket and slice thinly across the grain.
6. Skim excess fat from sauce and pour over brisket.
7. Serve on buns.

Deb's Tip:
Try texas toast instead of hamburger buns.

GOLDEN MUSHROOM BEEF

Ingredients:

2 tablespoons extra-virgin olive oil

2 pound eye of round steak, sliced 1-inch thick

1 teaspoon steak seasoning

2 medium onions, thinly sliced

1 teaspoon sugar

2 tablespoons red wine

1 package (8 ounces) button mushrooms, sliced

1 teaspoon beef bouillon

1 can (10¾ ounces) golden mushroom soup

Mashed potatoes

1. Rub steak slices with steak seasoning.
2. In a sauté pan, heat oil over medium heat.
3. Brown steak slices on both sides and transfer to crockery.
4. In the same pan, brown onions with sugar.
5. Add wine, mushrooms and bouillon to pan; sauté and transfer to crockery.
6. Pour mushroom soup into crockery. Cover.
7. Slow cook 5 hours on high or 10 hours on low.

Deb's Tip:
Serve with roasted garlic smashed potatoes.

CORNED BEEF AND CABBAGE

Ingredients:

1 corned beef brisket (2 to 2½ pound) with enclosed seasoning packet

8 medium red bliss potatoes, halved

6 large carrots, peeled and cut into 2-inch pieces

1 large sweet onion, quartered

1 cabbage, quartered

1 bottle (12 ounces) dark beer or ale

1 cup chicken or beef stock

1. Place all ingredients into crockery. Cover.
2. Slow cook 10 hours on low.

Deb's Tip:
Make sure you have malt vinegar and spicy
mustard in your pantry to serve with this dish.

MAMA'S STUFFED CABBAGE

Makes 6 servings

Ingredients:

1 large head of cabbage
1 pound extra-lean ground beef
½ cup onions, minced
1 teaspoon salt
1 teaspoon ground pepper
1 large egg, beaten

1 tablespoon Worcestershire sauce
1 cup rice, cooked
1 can (8 ounces) tomato sauce
1 tablespoon sugar
1 teaspoon beef stock
2 cups Mozzarella cheese, shredded

1. Separate cabbage into 12 large leaves.
2. Boil or steam cabbage until flexible, but not mushy. Drain and cool.
3. In a bowl, combine beef, onions, salt, pepper, egg and Worcestershire sauce.
4. Add rice to bowl. Mix well.
5. Place ¼ cup of beef mixture in the center of each cabbage leaf.
6. Fold in sides and roll ends over meat. Transfer to crockery.
7. In a bowl, combine tomato sauce, sugar and beef stock.
8. Pour over cabbage rolls. Cover.
9. Slow cook 2 hours on high or 4 hours on low.
10. Add Mozzarella cheese and cook until cheese is melted.

Deb's Tip:
For a low-fat alternative, substitute ground turkey for the beef and use quinoa instead of rice.

NO-BAKE LASAGNA

Makes 12 to 14 servings

Ingredients:

3 pounds ground beef

1 cup onions, diced

1 teaspoon garlic salt

1 teaspoon onion salt

½ teaspoon Italian seasoning

½ teaspoon ground pepper

1 can (28 ounces) petite, diced tomatoes with juice

2 jars (32 ounces) spaghetti sauce

Non-stick cooking spray

1 package (8 ounces) no-bake lasagna noodles

Cheese-Herb Mixture:

1 pound Mozzarella cheese, shredded

16 ounces Ricotta cheese

4 ounces Parmesan cheese, shredded

6 fresh basil leaves

2 large eggs, beaten

½ teaspoon salt

½ teaspoon ground pepper

1. In a sauté pan, brown meat and drain fat.
2. Add onions and cook until tender.
3. Add salts, Italian seasoning and pepper.
4. Add tomatoes with juice and spaghetti sauce. Heat thoroughly.
5. In a large bowl, combine cheese-herb mixture ingredients.
6. Spray crockery with non-stick spray.
7. Pour 2 cups of meat mixture into crockery and top with a layer of noodles.
8. Spread half the cheese-herb mixture and add a layer noodles.
9. Pour 1 cup of meat mixture over noodles.
10. Add remaining cheese-herb mixture and layer remaining noodles.
11. Top with meat mixture. Sprinkle with additional Parmesan. Cover.
12. Slow cook 3 hours on high or 6 hours on low.

SHEPHERD'S PIE

Makes 8 servings

Ingredients:

1 tablespoon extra-virgin olive oil

2 pounds ground beef

1 teaspoon onion salt

½ teaspoon ground pepper

½ cup onions, diced

½ cup celery, diced

½ cup carrots, diced

1 cup corn, canned or frozen

1 cup tiny frozen peas

2 cans (10¾ ounces each) golden mushroom soup

3 cups mashed potatoes

1. In a sauté pan, heat oil over medium heat.
2. Cook ground beef, drain fat and transfer to crockery.
3. Add salt, pepper, onions, celery, carrots and corn to crockery.
4. In a bowl, mix peas with mushroom soup and pour into crockery.
5. Top with mashed potatoes. Cover.
6. Slow cook 3 hours on high or 6 hours on low.

Deb's Tip:
To save time, buy ready-made mashed potatoes.

TAMALE PIE

Ingredients:

Non-stick cooking spray

2 pounds lean ground beef, cooked and drained

1 cup onions, diced

1 package chili seasoning

2 cans (28 ounces) tomatoes with green peppers

1 can (14 ounces) whole kernel corn, drained

1 can (2¼ ounces) sliced ripe olives, drained

1 package (16 ounces) corn bread mix

1 cup Cheddar cheese, shredded

1. Prepare corn bread mix according to box instructions.
2. Spray crockery with non-stick spray.
3. In a bowl, combine all ingredients, except batter and Cheddar cheese.
4. Transfer to crockery.
5. Pour batter into crockery. Top with cheese. Cover.
6. Slow cook 3 hours on high or 6 hours on low.

Deb's Tip:
As a variation, use ground pork or turkey instead of beef.

SANTA FE MEAT LOAF

CHILI PEPPERS & POWD

SENSATIONAL CINNAMO
Iona Keppler's Waffl
Fresh Strawberry C
Cynthia Lynn's Brea

W   YOU COOK FOR

Makes 10 to 1.

Ingredients:

2 cups torn soft bread, such as Challah, crusts removed

3 large eggs, beaten

1 cup salsa

1 teaspoon beef stock

3 pounds ground beef

½ cup onions, finely chopped

¼ cup cilantro, chopped

1 teaspoon taco seasoning

1 cup enchilada or taco sauce

1 cup Mexican cheese, shredded

1. In a large bowl, soak bread in eggs, salsa and stock.
2. Add ground meat, onions, cilantro and seasoning to bowl.
3. Line crockery with aluminum foil.
4. Form mixture into a loaf. Place into crockery. Cover.
5. Slow cook 4 hours on high or 8 hours on low.
6. Lift the foil, drain fat and return to crockery.
7. Top with sauce and cheese. Cover.
8. Slow cook for an additional 15 minutes on high until cheese is melted.

Deb's Tip:
Garnish with sour cream, lettuce,
Pico de Gallo and diced tomatoes.

OSSO BUCO

Ingredients:

2 tablespoons olive oil

2 to 2½ pounds veal shanks, cut crosswise into ½-inch pieces

2 tablespoons flour

1 teaspoon kosher salt

½ teaspoon ground pepper

1 can (14½ ounces) petite, diced tomatoes with juice

1 cup onions, diced

1 cup celery, chopped

½ cup carrots, chopped

2 garlic cloves, minced

1 cup beef stock

2 sprigs of thyme

Rice or orzo

1. In a sauté pan, heat oil over medium heat.
2. Coat veal shanks with flour and season with salt and pepper.
3. Brown veal on both sides and transfer to crockery.
4. Top with remaining ingredients, except rice or orzo. Cover.
5. Slow cook 4 hours on high or 8 hours on low.
6. Serve over rice or orzo.

Deb's Tip:
To save money, use beef or lamb shanks instead of veal shanks.

CHICKEN & TURKEY MEALS

Poultry With Passion...

LICKEDY-SPLIT LEMON CHICKEN

Ingredients:

4 pounds chicken, breasts or legs

2 teaspoons lemon-pepper seasoning

2 tablespoons olive oil

¼ cup onions, chopped

1 cup chicken stock

1 lemon, juice and zest

1 tablespoon fresh parsley, chopped

1 large sprig of thyme

¼ teaspoon paprika

2 teaspoons quick cook tapioca

1. Rinse chicken, pat dry and remove excess fat.
2. Rub liberally with lemon-pepper seasoning.
3. In a large sauté pan, heat oil over medium-high heat.
4. Add chicken and sear until golden brown. Transfer to crockery.
5. In the same pan, sauté onions until translucent. Transfer to crockery.
6. In a bowl, mix remaining ingredients. Pour over chicken. Cover.
7. Slow cook 2 hours on high or 4 hours on low.

Deb's Tip:
Serve with couscous and spinach.

MEDITERRANEAN CHICKEN

Makes 4 servings

Ingredients:

1 tablespoon olive oil

4 chicken breasts, boneless, skinless

1 teaspoon kosher salt

½ teaspoon ground pepper

1 teaspoon Italian herbs

3 garlic cloves, sliced

½ cup white wine

1 cup chicken stock

½ cup sun-dried tomatoes

1 can (14 ounces) artichoke hearts

½ cup black olives, pitted

1 can (10¾ ounces) cream of chicken soup

Pasta

1. Season chicken with salt, pepper and Italian herbs.
2. In a sauté pan, heat oil over medium heat.
3. Brown chicken on both sides and transfer to crockery.
4. Add remaining ingredients, except pasta. Cover.
5. Slow cook 2 hours on high or 4 hours on low.
6. Serve over pasta.

Deb's Tip:
For even more flavor, toss this with fresh pesto right before serving.

MOROCCAN CHICKEN

Ingredients:

2 tablespoons olive oil

1 whole chicken, cut into parts

½ teaspoon salt

½ teaspoon ground pepper

1 large onion, chopped

2 garlic cloves, minced

1 lemon, juice and zest

1 teaspoon paprika

¼ teaspoon ground turmeric

1 teaspoon quick cook tapioca

½ cup black olives

1 tablespoon fresh cilantro, chopped

1. Season chicken with salt and pepper.
2. In a large sauté pan, heat oil over medium-high heat.
3. Brown chicken on both sides. Transfer to crockery.
4. Add onions and garlic to crockery.
5. In a bowl, combine lemon, paprika, turmeric, tapioca and olives.
6. Pour mixture over chicken. Cover.
7. Slow cook 8 hours on low.
8. Sprinkle with cilantro. Serve.

CRUNCHY CHICKEN

Ingredients:

Non-stick cooking spray

½ cup mayonnaise

1 teaspoon poultry seasoning

½ teaspoon ground pepper

2 teaspoons fresh parsley, chopped

4 chicken breasts, boneless, skinless

1 cup grape nuts cereal

1. Spray crockery with non-stick spray.
2. In a bowl, combine mayonnaise, poultry seasoning, pepper and parsley.
3. Rub chicken with mixture.
4. On a plate, spread cereal.
5. Press each chicken breast into cereal until coated completely.
6. Transfer to crockery. Cover.
7. Slow cook 4 hours on high or 8 hours on low.

Deb's Tip:
I love to dice these up and serve them on a salad with buttermilk dressing.

SUNDAY-BEST TURKEY

Makes 8 servings

Ingredients:

5 pound turkey breast, skin and backbone removed

1 tablespoon salted butter, melted

1 teaspoon kosher salt

½ teaspoon poultry seasoning

1 teaspoon pepper

1 small onion, sliced

1 large carrot, sliced

2 celery stalks, sliced

3 sprigs of thyme

1. Rub turkey breast with butter.
2. Season with salt, poultry seasoning and pepper.
3. Place vegetables and thyme into crockery.
4. Top with turkey breast. Cover.
5. Slow cook 3 hours on high.

Deb's Tip:
The turkey stock in the crockery is an amazing foundation for a gravy.

FAR EAST CHICKEN

Ingredients:

6 chicken leg quarters

1 teaspoon dry Asian seasoning

1 tablespoon olive oil

½ cup soy sauce

¼ cup light brown sugar

1 garlic clove, crushed

1 tablespoon fresh ginger, grated

1 jar (6 ounces) hoisin sauce

1. Rinse chicken and pat dry.
2. Sprinkle with Asian seasoning.
3. In a large sauté pan, heat oil over medium heat.
4. Brown chicken on both sides and transfer to crockery.
5. In a bowl, combine remaining ingredients. Mix well.
6. Pour mixture into crockery. Cover.
7. Slow cook 4 hours on high or 8 hours on low.

Deb's Tip:
If you don't have hoisin sauce on hand, use a half cup of barbecue sauce instead.

CHICKEN & DUMPLINGS

Makes 6 to 8 servings

Ingredients:

Non-stick cooking spray

3 cups chicken, cooked and chopped

1 teaspoon salt

½ teaspoon ground pepper

2 cups carrots, sliced

½ cup celery, sliced

½ cup onions, diced

1 can (10¾ ounces) cream of chicken soup

1 can (10¾ ounces) cream of mushroom soup

1 can refrigerated buttermilk biscuits, quartered

1. Spray crockery with non-stick spray.
2. Place all ingredients into crockery, finishing with the biscuits. Cover.
3. Slow cook 2 hours on high or 4 hours on low.

Deb's Tip:
Substitute a 24-ounce bag of mixed frozen vegetables for the fresh ones.

CHICKEN ALA CANNES

FIND THE PENZEYS STORE
For even more stor
visit www.pe

Makes 4 s

Ingredients:

1 tablespoon extra-virgin olive oil

4 chicken breasts, skinless, bone-in

1 tablespoon Herbes de Provence

Pinch of salt and ground pepper

1 small onion, chopped

8 ounces mushrooms, sliced

1 cup chicken stock

1 can (10¾ ounces) cream of mushroom soup

1 box (8 ounces) petite peas

1 sprig of thyme

1. Rub chicken with Herbes de Provence.
2. In a sauté pan, heat oil over medium heat.
3. Brown chicken, bone-side up. Transfer to crockery.
4. In the same pan, cook onions and mushrooms for 3 minutes.
5. Add stock and soup to pan. Pour into crockery.
6. Add peas, thyme, salt and pepper to crockery. Cover.
7. Slow cook 2 hours on high or 4 hours on low.

PORK & SAUSAGE MEALS

Talk About Comfort Food...

APRICOT CHOP CHOPS

Makes 6 servings

Ingredients:

2 tablespoons salted butter

2 large onions, thinly sliced

8 ounces dried apricots

6 pork chops, 1-inch thick

1 teaspoon salt

½ teaspoon ground pepper

Apple pie spice

1 tablespoon prepared mustard

¼ cup chicken stock

2 tablespoons balsamic vinegar

2 tablespoons maple syrup

1 tablespoon cornstarch

2 tablespoons water

1. In a sauté pan, heat butter over medium heat.
2. Cook onions until browned. Transfer to crockery.
3. Add apricots to crockery.
4. Season pork with salt, pepper and spice.
5. In a sauté pan, brown chops and transfer to crockery.
6. In a bowl, mix mustard, stock, vinegar and syrup.
7. Pour mixture into crockery. Cover.
8. Slow cook 4 hours on high or 8 hours on low.
9. Dissolve cornstarch in water.
10. Transfer juices from crockery and cornstarch into a sauce pan.
11. Turn heat to medium and whisk until sauce comes to a boil.
12. When thickened, remove from heat.
13. Ladle sauce over pork chops.

Deb's Tip:
For a twist, try dried prunes or raisins instead of apricots.

TUSCAN PORK

Ingredients:

3 garlic cloves, chopped

3 sprigs of fresh rosemary leaves, chopped

2 teaspoons kosher salt

1 teaspoon ground pepper

1 teaspoon fennel seeds

¼ cup lemon juice

4 pound center-cut pork roast, bone-in

1 bag (10 ounces) frozen pearl onions

Pinch of crushed red pepper flakes

1. In a bowl, combine garlic, rosemary, salt, pepper and fennel seeds.
2. Pour lemon juice over pork.
3. Rub pork liberally with garlic-herb mixture. Cover. Refrigerate overnight.
4. The next day, place pork, bone-side down, into crockery.
5. Add onions, more salt, garlic mixture and red pepper flakes. Cover.
6. Slow cook 4 hours on high or 8 hours on low.

PORK ADOBADA

Ingredients:

8 dried whole chili peppers, chipotle or ancho

8 cups chicken stock

2 tablespoons tomato paste

5 pound pork loin, boneless, cut in 1-inch cubes

1 medium onion, diced

½ cup cider vinegar

½ cup orange juice

2 tablespoons brown sugar

6 garlic cloves, chopped

1 tablespoon ground cumin

Flour tortillas

1. Remove tops and seeds from dried chilies.
2. In a blender, purée chili peppers with chicken stock and tomato paste.
3. Place all ingredients, except tortillas, into crockery. Cover.
4. Slow cook 4 hours on high or 8 hours on low.
5. Serve with warm tortillas.

Deb's Tip:
To make a terrific chili, add beans, tomatoes and chili seasonings.

APPLE-CIDER PORK CHOPS

Makes 6 servings

Ingredients:

2 tablespoons olive oil

6 center-cut pork chops, boneless, 2-inches thick, butterflied

1 teaspoon salt

½ teaspoon ground pepper

¼ cup salted butter

1 large apple, cored and diced

1 package (6 ounces) corn bread stuffing

4 fresh sage leaves, chopped

2 cups apple cider

1 tablespoon apple cider vinegar

2 tablespoons chicken stock

1. In a large sauté pan, heat oil over medium-high heat.
2. Season pork with salt and pepper.
3. Brown pork on each side. Transfer to a platter.
4. Add butter to the pan and heat diced apples.
5. Add corn bread stuffing, sage and 1 cup of cider. Mix well.
6. Divide mixture between chops and transfer to crockery.
7. Pour remaining cider, stock and vinegar over chops. Cover.
8. Slow cook 4 hours on high or 8 hours on low.

Deb's Tip:
To add color, mix dried cherries into the stuffing.

SINGAPORE SOY-SAUCED RIBS

Ingredients:

4 pounds country-style pork ribs

½ teaspoon Chinese five-spice seasoning

1 jar (6 ounces) hoisin sauce

½ cup orange marmalade

¼ cup soy sauce

1 tablespoon rice wine vinegar

2 garlic cloves, minced

1 tablespoon freshly grated ginger or 1 teaspoon ginger powder

1. Place ribs into crockery.
2. In a bowl, mix remaining ingredients and pour over ribs. Cover.
3. Slow cook 4 hours on high or 8 hours on low.
4. Drain sauce from crockery into a saucepan.
5. Heat until sauce comes to boil to concentrate flavors.
6. Pour sauce over ribs.

DEB'S FAMOUS RIBS

Ingredients:

3 slabs of baby back ribs

1 lemon

3 teaspoons dry rib rub

Barbecue sauce

Dry Rib Rub:

1 tablespoon ground pepper

1 teaspoon cayenne pepper

2 tablespoons mild chili powder

2 tablespoons cumin

2 tablespoons dark sugar

2 tablespoons coriander seeds, crushed

4 tablespoons paprika

2 tablespoons salt

3 tablespoons celery salt

3 tablespoons garlic powder

1. Preheat broiler.
2. Cover a large broiler pan or baking sheet with aluminum foil.
3. Place ribs ,flesh-side down, in pan.
4. Using a sharp knife, make a slash through each rib membrane.
5. Broil 6 inches from heat, meat-side down, for 10 minutes.
6. Turn over ribs.
7. Squeeze with lemon juice and season with rub.
8. Broil for an additional 10 minutes.
9. Cut each slab in half and transfer to crockery. Cover.
10. Slow cook 3 hours on high or 6 hours on low.
11. Serve with barbecue sauce for dipping.

BBQ PULLED PORK

Ingredients:

4 pound fresh ham
1 teaspoon kosher salt
1 teaspoon garlic salt
1 teaspoon sweet paprika
1 teaspoon ground pepper
1 bottle (16 ounces) barbecue sauce
Sandwich rolls

1. Place ham, fat side up, into crockery. Cover.
2. Slow cook 10 hours on low.
3. Remove ham. Discard fat and bone.
4. Shred ham with a fork and return pork to crockery.
5. Add seasonings and barbecue sauce. Mix well.
6. Heat on warm setting.
7. Serve on sandwich rolls.

Deb's Tip:
For more crunch, add some coleslaw to the sandwich.

YBOR CITY PORK

Makes 12 to 14 servings

Ingredients:

5 pound pork loin, boneless, trimmed

2 cups sour orange juice

6 garlic cloves, chopped

1 tablespoon cilantro or oregano, chopped

1 teaspoon Latin seasoning

1. Place all ingredients into crockery. Cover.
2. Refrigerate over night.
3. The next day, slow cook 4 hours on high or 8 hours on low.
4. Serve with black beans and rice.

Deb's Tip:
If you can't find sour orange juice, just add the juice
of 2 limes to orange juice to make your own.

DESSERTS
Sweet Endings...

APPLE DAPPLE BAKE

Ingredients:

Non-stick cooking spray

8 Granny Smith apples, peeled, cored and sliced

1 lemon, juice and zest

½ cup dried cranberries

1½ cups sugar

1 teaspoon apple pie spice

½ cup unsalted butter, melted

Topping:

2 cups buttermilk baking mix

½ cup milk

3 tablespoons unsalted butter, melted

2 tablespoons brown sugar

1 cup granola

1. Spray crockery with non-stick spray.
2. In a bowl, combine apples, lemon, cranberries, sugar, spice and butter.
3. Transfer to crockery.
4. To make the topping, combine baking mix, milk, butter and brown sugar.
5. Mix until a dough forms.
6. Drop dough over apples using a spoon. Top with granola. Cover.
7. Slow cook 8 hours on low.

PEACH MELBA COBBLER

Makes 6 to 8 servings

Ingredients:

Non-stick cooking spray

4 cups peach slices, fresh or frozen

2 cups raspberries, fresh or frozen

1 orange, juice and zest, divided

1 cup sugar

Topping:

1½ cups buttermilk baking mix

3 tablespoons unsalted butter, melted

¼ cup milk

2 tablespoons sugar

1 teaspoon vanilla extract

1. Spray crockery with non-stick spray.
2. Layer peaches and raspberries in crockery.
3. Sprinkle with orange juice and top with sugar.
4. In a bowl, combine topping ingredients with orange zest.
5. Using a food processor, process until crumbly.
6. Sprinkle over fruit. Cover.
7. Slow cook 3 hours on low.

Deb's Tip:
Give it a kick by adding a half cup of peach brandy.

BERRY-GOOD RHUBARB CRISP

Makes 8 to 10 servings

Ingredients:

Non-stick cooking spray

5 cups rhubarb, chopped, fresh or frozen

3 cups strawberries, sliced, fresh or frozen

¾ cup sugar

2 teaspoons quick cook tapioca

Topping:

5 tablespoons unsalted butter

½ cup light brown sugar

½ cup flour

½ cup rolled oats

½ teaspoon apple pie spice

½ cup walnuts, chopped

1. Spray crockery with non-stick spray.
2. In a bowl, combine rhubarb, strawberries, sugar and tapioca.
3. Transfer to crockery.
4. To make the topping, place topping ingredients into a food processor.
5. Pulse 4 times. Avoid over-mixing the ingredients.
6. Sprinkle over fruit. Cover.
7. Slow cook 2 hours on high or 4 hours on low.
8. Serve warm with vanilla ice cream or cold with yogurt.

Deb's Tip:
In the summer, I love substituting blackberries for the strawberries.

PINA COLADA BREAD PUDDING

Ingredients:

Non-stick cooking spray

6 cups day-old French bread, cubed

½ cup dried pineapple, diced

4 large eggs, beaten

1 can (13½ ounces) coconut milk

1 can (15 ounces) cream of coconut

¼ cup dark rum

1. Spray crockery with non-stick spray.
2. In a large bowl, combine all ingredients. Mix well.
3. Transfer to crockery. Cover.
4. Slow cook 2 hours on high or 4 hours on low.

Deb's Tip:
Fill the bottom of a parfait glass with pineapple sundae topping. Add bread pudding, whipped cream and top with shredded coconut.

APPLE PECAN BREAD PUDDING

Makes 12 servings

Ingredients:

1 cup pecans, coarsely chopped

2 green apples, peeled, cored and sliced

1 cup sugar

1 teaspoon cinnamon

½ teaspoon nutmeg

3 large eggs

2 cups half-and-half or milk

¼ cup Bourbon

Non-stick cooking spray

8 slices raisin bread, diced

¼ cup unsalted butter, melted

1. Turn slow cooker to high.
2. Place pecans into crockery.
3. Toast pecans, uncovered, for 30 minutes. Stir occasionally.
4. Remove pecans from crockery.
5. In a bowl, mix sugar, cinnamon, nutmeg, eggs, half-and-half and Bourbon.
6. Spray crockery with non-stick spray.
7. Place bread, apples and pecans into crockery.
8. Pour egg mixture into crockery. Drizzle with butter. Cover.
9. Slow cook 4 hours on low until apples are tender and custard is set.
10. Turn off crockery and let bread pudding sit for an additional 15 minutes.

Deb's Tip:
Serve with hot maple syrup poured over the top.

EGGNOG BREAD PUDDING

Ingredients:

Non-stick cooking spray

3 large eggs

1 cup heavy cream

1 cup eggnog

½ cup sugar

½ cup dried cranberries

6 cups day-old French bread, cut into 1-inch cubes

2 tablespoons unsalted butter, cut into small pieces

½ teaspoon nutmeg, grated

Rum sauce

1. Spray crockery with non-stick spray.
2. In a large bowl, combine eggs, cream, eggnog, sugar and cranberries.
3. Add bread to egg mixture. Transfer to crockery.
4. Place butter pieces evenly across the top. Cover.
5. Slow cook 4 hours on low.

Deb's Tip:
Serve with my rum sauce, the recipe
is on the next page.

RUM SAUCE

Ingredients:

¾ cup sugar

1 tablespoon cornstarch

1 cup rum

1 tablespoon unsalted butter

1. In a bowl, combine sugar, cornstarch and rum.
2. Pour mixture into a saucepan and bring to a boil.
3. Add butter, let it melt and remove from heat.
4. Serve over bread pudding or other dessert.

FRUIT COMPOTE

Ingredients:

2 cups dried apricots

3 cups apricot nectar

½ cup dried cherries

½ cup sugar

2 teaspoons orange peel, grated

1. Place ingredients into crockery. Cover.
2. Slow cook 8 hours on low.

Deb's Tip:
This recipe makes an amazing topping
for French toast or bread pudding.

BLUEBERRY POUND CAKE

Ingredients:

1 package (16 ounces) pound cake mix
½ cup water
2 large eggs
1 cup frozen blueberries

1. Using an electric mixer, blend cake mix, water and eggs until moistened.
2. Gently fold in blueberries.
3. Pour batter into greased and floured 8-cup mold or springform pan.
4. Place into crockery. Top with 5 paper towels. Cover.
5. Slow cook 3 hours on high.

24-KARAT CAKE

Ingredients:

Non-stick cooking spray

6 large egg whites or ½ cup egg white substitute

½ cup fat-free yogurt

½ cup applesauce

1 teaspoon apple pie baking spice

1 package (2-layer size) spice cake mix

2½ cups carrots, shredded

½ cup dried raisins, chopped dried pineapple or apricots

¼ cup walnuts, chopped

1. Spray crockery with non-stick spray.
2. Using an electric mixer, mix all ingredients on low for 30 seconds.
3. Increase speed to medium and mix for an additional 2 minutes.
4. Transfer to crockery. Cover.
5. Slow cook 2 hours on high.
6. Invert cake onto a platter.
7. Top with my cream cheese frosting, the recipe is on the next page.
8. Cut into squares and serve.

Deb's Tip:
As a variation, try dried chopped pineapple or apricots instead of raisins.

CREAM CHEESE FROSTING

Ingredients:

1 package (8 ounces) fat-free cream cheese

¼ cup unsalted butter

2 teaspoons milk or cream

4 cups powdered sugar

1 teaspoon vanilla

1. In a food processor, mix ingredients until smooth and creamy.
2. Spread over cake.

Deb's Tip:
To make preparation easier, use cream cheese and butter at room temperature.

BERRY-CREAM CHEESE COFFEE CAKE

Makes 12 servings

Ingredients:

Non-stick cooking spray

1 package (8 ounces) cream cheese

2 tablespoons sugar

1 package (18¼ ounces) yellow cake mix

½ cup vegetable oil

4 large eggs

Filling:

1½ cups frozen mixed berries

2 tablespoons lemon juice

2 tablespoons sugar

1. Spray crockery with non-stick spray.
2. Using an electric mixer, blend cream cheese and sugar until smooth.
3. Add cake mix, oil and eggs.
4. Mix on low for 1 minute and then on high for an additional 2 minutes.
5. In a bowl, toss frozen berries, lemon juice and sugar.
6. Spread half of the cake batter evenly inside crockery.
7. Top with berry mixture.
8. Pour remaining cake batter over berry mixture. Cover.
9. Slow cook 2 hours on high.

FLOURLESS CHOCOLATE TORTE

Ingredients:

Non-stick baking spray with flour

6 large eggs, separated

1 cup powdered sugar

1½ sticks unsalted butter

9 ounces chocolate (containing 70% cocoa)

1 teaspoon vanilla extract

Pinch of salt

½ cup cherry or strawberry jam

1. Line an 8-inch cake pan with parchment paper and apply non-stick spray.
2. Fill crockery with 3 cups of boiling water and turn on high.
3. In a bowl, cream egg yolks with sugar until they turn a light yellow.
4. In a double boiler, melt butter and chocolate until smooth.
5. Slowly add chocolate to egg yolk mixture. Stir in vanilla and salt.
6. In a separate bowl, whisk egg whites until almost stiff peaks form.
7. Fold into chocolate mixture.
8. Transfer to pan and place into crockery. Cover.
9. Slow cook 2 hours on high or 4 hours on low. Remove.
10. Let cool for 30 minutes and invert onto cake stand.
11. Cut in half, spread with jam, and decorate with powdered sugar.

Deb's Tip:
Serve with my Chocolate Truffle Topping, the recipe is on page 151.

PEANUT BUTTER-COCOA CHEESECAKE

Makes 10 servings

Ingredients:

1 cocoa crust

24 ounces cream cheese, at room temperature

1 cup powdered sugar

¼ cup dark brown sugar

1 cup peanut butter

2 teaspoons vanilla extract

1 cup sour cream

Pinch of salt

4 large eggs

Chocolate Truffle Topping

1. Prepare cocoa crust; the recipe is on the next page.
2. In a food processor, purée all ingredients, except eggs, until smooth.
3. Add eggs, one at a time.
4. Pour batter into crust.
5. Wrap aluminum foil around the pan.
6. Pour 2 cups of water into crockery.
7. Place prepared springform pan into crockery. Cover.
8. Slow cook 2 hours on high.
9. Turn off crockery.
10. Let cheesecake sit for 1 hour inside slow cooker. Remove.
11. Top with chocolate truffle topping, the recipe is on page 151.
12. Let cake rest for 30 minutes before serving.

Deb's Tip:
Garnish with peanut butter cup candies.

COCOA CRUST

Ingredients:

Non-stick cooking spray

2 cups cocoa cereal

¼ cup unsalted butter

½ cup sugar

1. Cut parchment paper into a circle to fit the base of a 7-inch springform pan.
2. Secure ring over the base.
3. Spray pan liberally with non-stick spray.
4. Place all ingredients into a food processor fitted with a metal blade.
5. Pulse until cereal is crushed and ingredients are mixed.
6. Press into the pan.
7. Bake in oven for 10 minutes at 350 degrees.

CHOCOLATE TRUFFLE TOPPING

Ingredients:

¾ cup heavy cream

6 ounces dark chocolate, chopped

1. Pour cream into a 2 quart saucepan. Bring to a boil.
2. Remove from heat.
3. Add chocolate and whisk until smooth.
4. Let chocolate cool for 30 minutes.

Deb's Tip:
It is best to use high quality chocolate
containing at least 70% cocoa.

MOM'S RICE PUDDING

Ingredients:

Non-stick cooking spray

4 cups white jasmine rice, cooked

1 can sweetened condensed milk

2 cans (27 ounces each) coconut milk

1 cup raisins

1 teaspoon vanilla

1 teaspoon ground cinnamon

1. Spray crockery with non-stick spray.
2. In a bowl, mix cooked rice with condensed and coconut milk.
3. Transfer to crockery. Cover.
4. Slow cook 4 hours on low or until liquid is absorbed.
5. Stir in raisins and vanilla.
6. Sprinkle with cinnamon.

Deb's Tip:
If you like a thinner rice pudding, try adding a half cup of milk in the last half hour of cooking.

INDEX

For more of Deb's delicious ideas, please visit:
www.cookingwithdeb.com